# Collected Events

## Carol Garcia

Zeta Publishing
Ocala, FL

Copyright © 2012, 2018 Carol Garcia

All rights reserved. No part of this publication may be reproduced, distributed, or transmitted in any form or by any means, including photocopying, recording, or other electronic or mechanical methods, without the prior written permission of the publisher, except in the case of brief quotations embodied in critical reviews and certain other noncommercial uses permitted by copyright law. For permission requests, write to the publisher, addressed "Attention: Permissions Coordinator," at the address below.

Zeta Publishing, Inc
3850 SE 58th Ave
Ocala, FL 34480
www.zetapublishing.com

This is a work of fiction. All of the characters, names, incidents, organizations, and dialogue in this novel are either the products of the author's imagination or are used fictitiously.

Ordering Information:
Quantity sales. Special discounts are available on quantity purchases by corporations, associations, and others. For details, contact the publisher at the address above.
Orders by U.S. trade bookstores and wholesalers. Please contact Zeta Publishing: Tel: (352) 694-2553; Fax: (352) 694-1791 or visit www.zetapublishing.com

First Published by Xlibris

Rev. Date: 5/18/2018

ISBN: 978-1-947191-88-4 (sc)

ISBN: 978-1-947191-89-1 (e)

Library of Congress Control Number: 2018945332

Printed in the United States of America

# Texas, My Dream

By Carol A. Garcia, 1963

Our nation could not stand
or be as proud or great,
To share the glory of victory
without the Lone Star State.

Texas may have many things
from trees to rolling plains,
Including deserts and mountains
and some unexplored terrains.

I'm aware of its many riches
from cattle to black gold,
With cowboys tall in courage
boasting of tales so bold.

Your state, considered the greatest
and perhaps will always be,
But what's missing in Texas
is the total presence of me.

# Attitude Is Everything

By Carol A. Garcia, September 1994

Your attitude is everything; it shows me who you are.
If you're hateful, mad, or angry, you're always ready to spar.
The attitude that's positive and pleasant is right on base,
Expressing a peaceful nature with a glowing happy face.
If for some reason your feelings get ruffled or sore,
Before entering my classroom, park that attitude at the door.

# Stolen Moments

Since I've met you, I have joy in my heart,
A promise of pleasure, until we're to part.

From the tone of your voice, to the touch of your hands,
You excite my whole body, with your alluring demands.

Your kisses so sweet, I just melt in your arms,
Your touch is so soft, I give into your charms.

You're gentle and patient, so confident with pride,
I'm confused so completely, I couldn't resist if I tried.

I can't talk or think right, I'm almost a fright,
You thrill me to pieces, with your look of delight.

You said you'll not hurt me, but I think it's too late,
Of stolen moments together, I love it when we mate.

# I Am a Tree

By Carol A. Garcia

I live in the forest, I am a tree,
I'm never lonely, animals visit with me.

The birds nest in my branches and hide in my leaves,
to raise their young and to launch in the breeze.

A badger digs in the ground beneath my outer roots,
to stay away from the hunter that shoots.

In my trunk live the squirrels, insects, and coons,
and at night some animals feed by the moon.

The deer pass me by and hide where they can,
to evade being stalked by their enemy—man.

My leaves shade the ground, I give comfort to all,
except during the seasons of winter and fall.

I stabilize the soil on the rolling hills and plains,
I help stop the erosion to the streams when it rains.

To grow, I use water, the soil, and the sun,
and my by-products are enjoyed by man for fun.

I add beauty to the scenery, oxygen to the air,
it's my way of balancing nature and doing my share.

My manager is the forester, all educated and bright,
to keep a renewable resource, from disappearing from sight.

# To One of Kilgore's Finest

*By Carol A. Garcia*

To a guy named Richard, the resource officer to our schools,
He wears a badge and gun, while enforcing the golden rules.

He encourages our youth to be completely free of drugs,
By supporting our KYSSED program and arresting the thugs.

He talks to our students and to our classes brings info,
If you're approached to take drugs, you just say no.

He's friendly and pleasant, so courageous and bright,
In his uniform of dark blue, he's a handsome sight.

This officer of ours, around Kilgore, is well known,
He works security at other businesses on loan.

We appreciate you, Richard, for coming to us this day,
For informing us of the law and order way.

A man of many virtues, so honorable and true,
We salute you, Officer Stanley, for what you do.

# Ballad of "Jimmy Rich"

By Carol A. Garcia, February 23, 1982

Situated on the equator in an even temperature belt,

Where the mouth of the Amazon River opens to its continental shelf.

A man must keep his vigil in this lonely and desolate place,

Surrounded by steel and water to a life not always safe.

For on an offshore drilling rig he stays for twenty-eight days,

To put in time of sweat and work for the enormous money it pays.

By using his mind of technology, he secures the precious black gold,

For he lives in the heavens near Taurus on the (giant hunter) Orion, I'm told.

And when this man comes stateside back to the good ole USA,

He collects memories of love and home with pleasurable moments of play.

This life with its measurable certainty is as good as it can be,

But what's missing on the drilling rig Orion is the total presence of me.

## What Will Santa Bring?

At Kilgore High School, it's Christmastime,
With seasonal decorations so fine.

Santa could bring you a deserving award,
It might be high tech so you won't get bored.

It could be a necklace or a smell so sweet,
Or maybe a Ty Baby to complete your treat.

This gift of goodies includes something great,
To help make your Christmas holidays first rate.

# My Lord and Master

By Carol A. Garcia, February 1991

Don't take your eyes off Jesus, don't ever go astray,
Don't take your eyes off Jesus, for heaven is yours one day.

You're a mighty soldier for the Lord, with the belt of truth at your waist,
Armed with his spiritual gifts, they reflect joy to your face.

You're wearing the helmet of salvation and dressed in the armor of God,
So girt up your loins for battle using the mighty Spirit of the sword.

Your shield will resist all the fiery darts shot by the evil one,
With the gospel of peace as your footgear, salvation is through his Son.

So keep your eyes on Jesus, let his love brighten your day,
He'll protect and keep you safe with the Spirit, he'll guide your way.

# Global Effects

By Carol A. Garcia, 1995

A gal named Sally went into space,
Launched from Kennedy, it wasn't a waste.

From cameras a many, the photos she snapped,
Aimed at the air, sea, land, and mountains a capped.

She's now a teacher in Southern Cal,
Where she does research and physics, what a gal!

With a Global Change Workshop given at Caltech,
As forty US teachers came to learn of this effect.

We listened to lectures and developed our notes,
We met deadlines, took field trips, and discovered new hopes.

We're proud to be here in this beautiful state,
With this new knowledge, we'll change the earth's fate.

# Upcoming Events

*By Carol A. Garcia*

I wonder if you truly know how much we all love you,
Which includes your inner self and your sexy smile so true.

Our existence will not be exciting until your presence is here,
We need your charm, wit, and humor, in our daily lives so near.

You're soon to grace our company, living in Longview so great,
Your past is gone, your time is up, freedom at last to live your own fate.

The road will not be easy, many disappointments may come your way,
But with determination and a positive attitude, success will make your day.

Some people may not be nice or give you the chance you seek,
But work you'll find, and gratitude you'll show as joy of the meek.

Put God as your top priority, he'll guide you through your life,
With his spirit, grace, and Word and my daughter as your wife.

# The Sentinel

By Carol A. Garcia

I miss you in your corner,
standing so brave and tall.

Watching for infractions while
guarding the eighth grade hall.

I miss our daily talks,
between classes and at lunch,

And watching the halls closely
so the kids won't bunch.

But most of all I miss you,
drinking coffee from your mug,

With your spirit-lifting actions
and friendly daily hugs.

# Learning Can Be Fun

By Carol A. Garcia

Learning to use a computer can be lots of fun,
Experimenting and playing programs that run.

A PowerPoint is an outline of lessons to use,
It makes learning orderly of material not to lose.

I've learned to use a spreadsheet, it's a real treat,
For numbers, columns, and data kept neat.

I've enjoyed this workshop, it's been a blast,
Of knowledge needed for the time to pass.

# Our Shining Knight

By Carol A. Garcia

To a man named Derrick, the truant officer of our schools,
He wears a badge and a gun while enforcing the golden rules.

In his afternoon duties, he's patrolling our city streets,
By serving the public and performing various other feats.

He encourages our youth to be completely free of drugs,
By supporting our KYSSED program and arresting the thugs.

He'll talk to your students and to the class he'll show,
If approached to take drugs, just how to say no.

He loves to go fishing on a lake so crystal clear,
While prowling the woods in the season of the deer.

He's friendly and pleasant, so courageous and bright,
In his uniform of dark blue, he's a handsome sight.

We appreciate you, Derrick, for coming to us this day,
For bringing us knowledge of the law and order way.

A man or many virtues, so honorable and true,
We salute you, Officer Robertson, for what you do.

# A Tribute to Michael

By Carol A. Garcia

To a guy named Michael, who wears a badge and a gun,
He makes his living riding in a county squad car for fun.

Protecting the innocent and arresting the thugs,
Especially those who break the law using drugs.

Well organized and secure in the law enforcement field,
He's honest and trusting, so beware criminals: no deals!

To the county jail you'll go if a bad deed you've done,
It's a place of punishment where your freedom is taken from.

So courageous and brave, this man does his duty,
In his uniform of tan, he's rated quite a cutie.

We appreciate you, Michael, for coming on this day,
For bringing us knowledge of the law and order way.

A man of many talents, with the highest principles too,
We salute you, Deputy Ferguson, for what you do.

# Gregg County's Finest
By Carol A. Garcia, November 5, 1996

To our handsome new sheriff, a guy named Les,
He won with a write-in election 'cause he was the best.

He ran his campaign on the issues of today,
Stressing his leadership, respect, and truthful ways.

Experienced as a cop, with a master's degree too,
He's a teacher of the law, with integrity and loyalty so true.

He's a fair and honest man, he'll treat the people right,
With the county's interest in mind, he'll work for unity with insight.

By the spiritual touch of God, his visions will come to pass,
If our county is to grow in the trusting ways that last.

Alex, Chase, and Jackie, he's a father to these three,
His mate's name is Pam, and he's as happy as can be.

The challenge of golf is the game he likes to play,
A place to relax, have fun after a hard workday.

So to our new sheriff, who's courageous, smart, and bright,
We salute you, Les Ferguson, who will always do what's right.

# To David and Guy

By Carol A. Garcia, 1996

To a cop named David, and his wonder dog, Guy,
Who will arrest you for drugs if you're on the buy.

He makes his living wearing a badge and a gun,
While Guy sniffs lockers, cars, and buildings for fun.

Well organized and secure, he enforces all the laws,
He drives a squad car and will stop you for a cause.

To the jailhouse you'll go if a bad deed you've done,
It's a place of confinement, no freedom and no fun.

He's outgoing and friendly, plus courageous and brave,
Handsome in his uniform, certain gals have known to rave.

We appreciate you both for coming on this day,
For bringing us knowledge of the law and order way.

A man of multiple talents, with the highest principles too,
We salute you, Officer Falco, for what you do.

# To One of Gregg County's Finest

By Carol A. Garcia, 1996

We miss you, Floyd, from our school,
Walking the halls, enforcing the rules.

We miss your smile, your badge, and your gun,
Your charismatic contact with the student for fun.

You're brave, strong, courageous, and bright,
In your uniform of tan, you're a handsome sight.

Fishing for bass, on a lake crystal clear,
Is your favorite pastime, catching food so dear.

You've shown us the way by living your beliefs,
If you continue this practice, some day you'll be chief.

We applaud you, Floyd, for being honest and true,
We salute you, Officer Wingo, for what you do.

As a final good-bye from all your teacher friends,
With love and affection to you we all send.

# The American Soldier

By Carol A. Garcia

Common folk make up the military of the USA,
Who protect our nation and its Constitution in every way.

Be any branch of the service, our GIs are great,
They're our pride and joy and are considered top rate.

In fields a many, with training and education courses,
They become our nation's elite fighting forces.

Known as GIs, they will travel the world around,
To be on duty where injustice might be found.

Being number 1, our troops are always first to fight,
Guided by the Holy Spirit, the USA will do what's right.

# How We Touch the Future

By Carol A. Garcia

A flower garden is a beautiful place,
For each bud and blossom has a different face.

With leaves and stems and the many shades of green,
Some forms are bulky, and some forms are lean.

Each blossom has color, all different but bright,
It's a mixed rainbow and an awesome sight.

This garden is my classroom, a treasure so rare,
I tend to it daily with special, special care.

The flowers represent the students in my classes,
With TLC and knowledge to increase their brain masses.

Some students work hard, for class rank they aim high,
While others come to play, later regretting they didn't try.

Many days are full of sunshine, a few are cloudy or wet,
No matter who the student is, I'm glad we've met.

Some students grow slowly, and some grow fast,
But with each six weeks, they all hope to pass.

I have touched their future in this garden of mine,
And with the Holy Spirit, they'll all mature in time.

# His Journey of Faith

By Carol A. Garcia, July 1997

On this August day, we honor Father Marty,
In celebration with a three-day party.

The guests are all here, along with his clan,
With activities of joy to acknowledge this man.

A priest he became some forty-five years ago,
When he answered God's call of the gospel to sow.

In the military he went to proclaim God's Word,
Which renewed men's faith whenever they heard.

He took on evangelization in the area of St. Paul,
To excite the Spirit where souls claimed the call.

I thank the Lord for knowing this man,
Who's touched my life with his loving hand.

He's gentle and kind, soft spoken and sweet,
With a twinkle in his eye that makes him unique.

He's retiring this month to relax and to rest,
To set God's examples as to how to live best.

So great is his love for the Lord God above,
On his journey to heaven, he'll be guided by a dove.

# "My Shadow"

By Carol A. Garcia, October 1998

To this kid named Chris, "my shadow" became he,
A student from school in my class he wanted to be.

Every morning he greeted me to begin each day,
Between classes and after school seeking direction of his way.

He's a bright young man, intelligent and smart.
Any career of his choice will come from his heart.

His aim is to be president of this country so great,
Or even a CIA member that just might be his fate.

Bryce Brown, his friend, in the navy wants to be,
To serve his country and the whole world to see.

An invite to worship at the church of Christ the King,
He joins in with the choir as the Spirit moves him to sing.

His mentor is Father Mark, our local parish priest,
Who demonstrates through his actions God's way of serving the least.

His soul has been fed; he's filled with God's grace,
Expressing joy and love with a smiling, happy face.

Chris is no longer "my shadow" as you can plainly see,
But a soldier for the Lord as a future priest to be.

## Never Ever Again

By Carol A. Garcia, July 25, 1999

I've been behind these bars, I'm never coming back,
To ever again break the law or to get off track.

This place made me realize, my direction's not right,
So I changed my attitude when I finally saw the light.

As the days went by, learning became my ambition,
It improved my mind and strengthened me as a Christian.

I studied for a GED, the HVAC, and took a Narda test,
All completed and passed, I did my extra best.

My future's bright now, like the rising morning sun,
I'll join my new family with my own life to run.

With my beautiful bride-to-be, Trinity Ann is her name,
She brightens my very soul and keeps my mind sane.

Forever supportive, my parents were always there,
With encouragement, letters, and visits saying, "We care."

My new adopted mom helped to raise my self-esteem,
She became my inspiration and challenged me to dream.

I've served my time here, I'm finally free at last,
Now to put this experience deep in my past.

I'm never coming back here, no never ever again,
With my faith in the Holy Spirit and the guidance he'll send.

# His Journey of Opportunity

By Carol A. Garcia, 2000

This special man from Lebanon, to the USA came he,
To this land of opportunity, to see what he could be.

From the University of Texas, he earned his PhD.
In all the natural sciences, an expert became he.

Working at TEA gave him contacts across the state,
Advising and directing teachers to help them become first rate.

On an accreditation visit in '87, I met this handsome man.
He came to my room, looked at plans, and extended a helping hand.

With a wife, a son, and two daughters, his family is complete,
Displaying joy and happiness that can't be beat.

For fun and relaxation, growing roses became his passion.
Someday a rare beauty may evolve as a main attraction.

Highly skilled in chemistry, he teaches a college class,
Challenging young people to reach excellence, not just to pass.

He now heads the Regional Collaborative of this great state,
So teachers will get trained in science that's up to date.

Our fearless leader, Kamil A. Jbeily, inspires every teacher,
By challenging them to goals where hands-on is the main feature.

Blessed by the Lord, he can create and see visions,
With guidance from the Holy Spirit, he'll make the right decisions.

America is the land of the proud, the brave, and the free,
Because where else would opportunity like this be?

# A Salute to Science

By Carol A. Garcia, July 21, 2001

In '90–'91, a reform was sweeping this great state,
By changing obsolete methods for learning that's up to date.

All over Texas, regional clusters did meet,
To adopt new science methods that can't be beat.

A support system for education became its main link,
By sharing ideas, making connections, and getting kids to think.

Out of these concepts the Texas Collaborative was born,
A state-supported program to advance the new reform.

The State of Texas has twenty educational service centers,
It's a program where teachers can get help from mentors.

This special group includes over seven thousand educators statewide,
They implement knowledge for TAKS and create labs on the side.

In the year 2000, the state recognized this program as being number 1.
It was inducted into the Texas Science Hall of Fame for learning made fun.

Our director, Kamil A. Jbeily, gives inspiration to all,
By using hands-on experiments and making science a ball.

The future of this program is for every teacher to be,
Using up-to-date science for this new knowledge is the key.

Because of this collaborative, our science classes are top rate,
It's one of the things that make Texas so great.

# Principal's Pride

By Carol A. Garcia, June 6, 2002

Janel, it doesn't seem quite right,
the principal you'll not be.
To lead St. Mary's faculty,
plus your harassment towards me.

You take on another position,
as a teacher no less.
You'll be joining the working ranks,
along with the very best.

I've always admired you,
long faculty meetings and all,
'Cause you're a dedicated educator,
with a caring, loving call.

This little gift is for you,
use it wisely with pride,
So you'll remember me always,
I was the "thorn in your side."

# In Memory of Luke

By Carol A. Garcia, April 2003

In the early years, his ability was easy to see,
With a special talent for sports, a leader was he.

Luke was smart and witty, also liked a lot,
As a student in my class, a clown he was not.

He brightened my room with his smiling face,
With so many friends, no matter their race.

His joyous laughter was contagious in class,
With his dynamic personality, the time went fast.

To all who knew him, he will be greatly missed,
And his memory remains at the top of our list.

Although a tragedy to us it may seem,
Maybe God needed Luke to play on his team.

# A Nation United

By Carol A. Garcia, September 2003

Our way of life changed on the eleventh of September,
A day of tragedy we will long remember.

With violent cowardly acts al-Qaida seeks our downfall,
Using jets as bombs, they hit the Towers' walls.

George W. Bush, the president of the USA,
Has promised the American people the terrorists will pay.

In this time of crisis, our people remained strong,
Because our leader stood his ground and said, "That's wrong!"

With faith and confidence this emergency was handled right,
He listened to his advisors, then thought through the fight.

Bush talked to the nation, his decision was finally made,
What plan of action to take, to get justice for this raid.

Our civil servants were the heroes, so brave and bold,
They bonded together and displayed courage untold.

We are a peaceful nation, our land is strong and free,
With opportunities galore and dreams yet to be.

Everywhere you go, ole glory's on display,
It assures freedom and justice for its people every day.

To our commander in chief, these words I repeat,
"With the Holy Spirit, America will never know defeat."

# Toward the Second Mile

By Carol A. Garcia, June 25, 2004

To Nita Beth, well done, for your service of many years.
Your presence will truly be missed, the envy of all your peers.

From teacher to a science coordinator, your experiences are too many to tell,
Perfect as a role model for educators, a pattern that's worked so well.

You've done workshops and conferences all over this state,
Your creativity has helped to make Texas become first rate.

Hands-on is the way to teach, to learn, and to retain the facts,
It helps students recall for the test, taking TEKS.

In the battle for your life, you never got riled.
Uplifted by the Holy Spirit reflecting God's smile.

Your friend Dr. V helped you get through this,
With new treatments, and drugs and prayers added to lists.

Tom, your husband, has been there for you,
Through him your strength was always renewed.

You are now a part-time consultant who will work only once in a while,
To help teachers in need of activities that you keep tucked in your files.

Now you have time for things you want to do,
Visiting friends and family and grandchildren too.

Nita Beth, my special friend and mentor, a person with courage untold,
Personality, character, and a spirit-filled life
Those are the memories of you I will hold!

# Across the Years

By Carol A. Garcia, May 19, 2005

To my wonderful sister Patricia,
who's my friend and best pal,
We grew up on a Wisconsin farm
with memories too numerous to tell.

Our education started at Maple School,
a mile and a quarter away,
It was a one-room schoolhouse
where we walked to and from every day.

During recess, Rook was a popular card game,
or a ball game against another school,
We played and worked together
to learn the golden rule.

Living on a farm is not always fun,
we learned early what had to be done,
We picked cucumbers during the summer
and milked cows, which was really a bummer.
In the Omro High School band,

Pat played the saxophone,
She marched in parades and tournaments
and played everything in perfect tone.

We had many summer jobs
because college wasn't free,
We worked in canning factories,
wax companies, and tutored for a fee.

A graduate of UW at Oshkosh,
with a library science degree,
She entered the workforce
for a difference in the world to be.

My sister was the traveler,
she experienced many places,
From Alaska, Japan, and Germany,
she always met new faces.

Pat was my role model growing up,
my roomie and playmate too,
Always filled with God's Spirit and love,
she's my favorite sister sent from above.

# Life in Rural Wisoncin

1930-1963        By Carol Basel Garcia, June 2009

Life on the farm wasn't all work
sometimes as a family we had fun,
Special occasions as rare as they were
from holidays to playing in the sun.

There were fourteen kids in all
eight boys and the girls were six,
Ma and Pa were married once before
bringing to the new union a wonderful mix.

Six of our brothers served in the navy.
Ed, Donald, Norbet, and Eddie in WWII,
Kenneth in the Korean conflict and Tommy in peace time
But all served with honor to keep America true.

Our education began at Maple School
a mile and a quarter away,
It was a one-room schoolhouse for eight grades
of which we walked to and from every day.

We learned our ABCs, did math, studied history
and followed the golden rule,
During recess we played Rook, Simon says, baseball
and competitive games against other schools.
During the summers we were never idle
we made money picking cucumbers and beans,
As we grew older, the Green Giant Canning Companies
helped pay college tuitions to complete our dreams.

Our father never worried about help on the farm
we milked cows, fed animals, and picked rocks from fields,
My sister Pat got excused from barn chores
when getting ringworm on her hand, she helped Ma with meals.

Mother had a veggie garden every year
plus fruit trees and lots of flowers,
She would can, freeze, put up jellies
and toil in the kitchen for hours.

Harvest time was always a big deal
from haying, filling silos, or thrashing wheat,
Neighborhood farmers brought tractors, wagons, and horses
to finish the work for a deadline to meet.

Every Saturday was housecleaning time
when we dusted, cleaned, and scrubbed floors,
Each girl would take a room
to quickly complete her given chores.

On holy days and Saturdays we attended church
and learned about our religion after Mass,
The afternoons were spent seeing a movie
when for 25¢ we viewed big screen casts.

Winters were cold, dreary, and long
we burned wood and coal for heat,
Sometimes we built castles of snow
to play games with our brothers to beat.

There was always a school Christmas program
and a stage built of planks over bailed hay,
Each child had an acting part
for families to brag on in a big way.

And then we moved to a larger house
with a larger barn and land,
We attended a big public school
rode the bus and joined the high school band.

But we turned out all right
some completed college to make their way,
With God's graces and his Holy Spirit
we put into practice our faith today.

# A Tribute to Greg Brown

By Carol A. Garcia, December 2008

This man from East Texas, to our town comes he,
To explore the opportunity as to what he could be.

In a variety of subjects this material he well knows,
With history and sports being what he chose.

A family man is he, with kids and a wife,
He's proud of his achievements; this enjoyment is his life.

As an A&M graduate and a former head coach too,
He came to Kilgore High School as our principal anew.

Greg met with teachers and asked for their insight,
He established new methods to set some old rules right.

He interacts with the kids, being friendly to all,
Performing many duties and making important calls.

As for us teachers, we're happy he's at our school,
Blessed by the Holy Spirit, he will enforce the Golden Rule.

# My Black Hills Vacation

(Collette Style)            By Carol A. Garcia, July, 2011

With the 1880 train ride my adventure began,
From Hill City to Keystone through the Black Hills it ran.

The ponderosa pine with its many shades of green,
Stand majestically and strong in the Black Hills scene.

Mount Rushmore was next to see with the presidents of four,
The faces of George, Thomas, Abe, and Teddy for events completed and more.

On day 2 the developing statue of Crazy Horse I saw,
Where blasts of granite rock and dust did fall.

Many animals roam at Custer State Park, from bison to the bighorn sheep,
To live and not fear man in their environment to reap.

The next stop was at a gold outlet store to see leafy detailed jewelry so fine,
From rings, watches, and necklaces all shiny and smooth as wine.

A famous city: Deadwood, where Wild Bill was shot,
Buried next to Calamity Jane and visited by tourist a lot.

Tatanka, the mighty bison have their story dramatically told,
In *Dances with Wolves*, with Kevin Costner, who is sympathetically bold.

I experienced the Wild Horse Sanctuary, my favorite site,
I saw wild colts and horses plus equine facts a right.

The Lakota Indian Reservation was on the program to see,
In much need of repair is the Memorial of Wounded Knee.

I experienced from local town places cuisine so fine.
The Bay Leaf Café and K Bar S Lodge, a few that come to mind.

My vacation ended at Mount Rushmore at night.
To see the lighting of presidents and hearing music so right.

# Becca Boo

By Carol Garcia, December 2011

To Stepping Stones this child went
to master her ABCs.
She's bright, smart, and witty
as learning became a breeze.

Her elementary days were at St. Mary's
a Longview Catholic School,
Making friends and delighting
in learning the golden rule.

High school was special in Kilgore
while excelling in many deeds,
Being second in the class with encouragement
to a TCU scholarship it leads.

Soccer was her sport of choice
a game she frolicked in fun,
Playing in private clubs, high school
and college, it kept us on the run.

In Peru she spent a year
in the Andes Mountains so wild,
Searching for varieties of orchids
and new species to compile.

In January on a beach in Mexico
Becca and Cole were wed,
With family and friends in attendance
and congratulations were said.

Of our daily, nightly chats
I miss having them with you
Sharing ideas of girl stuff
and discussing things to do.

A medical doctor she'll become
whose future is promising and bright
With the Holy Spirit to guide her
launching a career in blessed might.

# The Crown Prince

By Carol A. Garcia, December 2011

Gregory, the crown prince
with a personality that's first rate,
He's gentle, witty, and smart
with a future filled with blessed fate.

For learning numbers, colors, and shapes
to Stepping Stones he was sent,
Where he played games with friends
and recalling only things that meant.

Next came St. Mary's Catholic School
from the first to eighth grade
He was active in many sports
enjoying all the teams he made.

For high school he chose Longview
where he excelled in all his classes,
And playing computer games with friends
his way for time passing.

A TCU scholarship he was awarded
to further his interest in psych,
He's now working on his doctorate
with a future that's bright and right.

The sport he loves is soccer
the game keeps him agile and fit,
Playing in a league for fun
to keep up his charm and wit.

Greg adopted a dog named Hershey
a mutt he found roaming free,
He loves this dog and trained her
as his comrade to be.

Shaping the minds of our youth
will be this college professor's aim,
With the Holy Spirit to guide him
this project will lead to fame.

# A Journey to Faith

By Carol A. Garcia, April 10, 2012

I met this gal many years ago
taking classes at Tyler's UT,
She was finishing her educational degree
and a certificate to teach for me.

We hit it off right away
with kids and us being divorced,
Her three daughters were young
my daughter a teen, a son a grader fourth.

Both our exes dumped us
just left us high and dry,
Leaving broken hearts and scars
to mend as the time goes by.
We both went different ways
being in the field of education,
I taught geography to ninth graders
while Sally pursued the elementary ones.

We always kept in contact
via letters, e-mails, or the phone,
And the years hurried by fast
children maturing, in college, or leaving home.

Finally, Sally settled in Austin
where she met a guy named Joe,
But her faith in God never waned
as the Holy Spirit continues to grow.

Today we pray for our children
grandkids, sons-in-laws, and mates,
We've been blessed abundantly by the Lord
to give praise and thanks for our holy fate.

# "Liner" Profit

By Carol A. Garcia, March 19, 2012

I need to tell you a story about this wonderful gal,
I met some years ago who became my teacher pal.

We conversed daily for strength and encouragement,
It enlightened the chaos of details the Ivory Tower sent.

What I admire most about this agile "she",
Is her love for Jesus's virtue being the perfect key.

This lady is friendly and nice displaying a nature of peace.
By showing God's love sometimes to the very least.

www.ingramcontent.com/pod-product-compliance
Lightning Source LLC
Chambersburg PA
CBHW071543080526
44588CB00011B/1775